Igbo Voices; hidden wisdom from the ancient language.

Igbo Voices

Igbo Voices; hidden wisdom from the ancient language.
Igbo Voices

Understand Africa, Understand your world.

Uzoma Nwosu M.D.

New York, New York.

Igbo Voices; hidden wisdom from the ancient language.

Note to the reader; this book is not intended as a substitute for medical advice or treatment.

I recommend that you have a dictionary handy. Always check up any word you do not fully understand in any Standard English dictionary.

Igbo Voices; hidden wisdom from the ancient language.

Contents

Igbo Voices; hidden wisdom from the ancient language.

Igbo voices

Igbo Voices; hidden wisdom from the ancient language.

Acknowledgements.

Many thanks to Mr. Michael B. Daniels, Ufuoma Otu, and Richard Brown M.D.

I also thank my parents, grandparents and Igbo predecessors.

Igbo Voices; hidden wisdom from the ancient language.
Preface

There is considerable genetic, archeological and paleontological evidence that language most probably first developed, during the middle stone age, in sub-Saharan Africa. It is however unclear, how these early languages transformed into our current complex language systems.

Language is a means in which a people communicate their internal and external experiences. Words can be used to capture the truth about the observations a people make in their physical universe. By looking at each word, we could be examining their 'truth' as they have observed it.

I undertook this assignment after the realization that ancient Igbo words contain certain commands or actions in them. As I further examined the words, I began to realize these words must have been created by a very complex ancient civilization.

Most importantly, I concluded that the examination of these words have great relevance in the modern world.

Looking at the Igbo word for Law 'Iwu', we can readily identify the root word as 'wu'. But what is 'wu'? To understand what that root 'wu' communicates, let's look at other words containing the same root. One is owu, which is used to describe the agony or distress an individual experiences when they are short of money or funds. The other word is nwute which is long suffering or prolonged agony an individual can experience due to a number of conditions. Notice that the verb te in nwute is communicating a 'prolonged' event. So we can translate that verb wu as agony or distress. We will find out later that the I in Iwu is a root or verb intensifier. So we can translate Iwu(law) as **agonizing**.

Igbo Voices; hidden wisdom from the ancient language.
In Igbo speech, when an individual violates the law, we say 'Iwu a ma go gi' which actually reads 'the law has known you' or 'agony has known you'. So the 'internal action' experienced by breaking the law is agony.

These words are communicated by the same root or verb for a specific purpose. When one breaks the law(i**wu**), not only would there be agony, there would be o**wu**(agony due to lack of funds/means), and then n**wu**te(prolonged suffering). The purpose is synergism.

Interest in the origin of words is rising. The word hippopotamus is actually of ancient Greek origin from hippos potamios, literally, riverine horse. This clarification throws understanding into the timeline when the ancient Greeks first encountered and named this animal, and how it eventually became an English word.

Understanding Igbo words, their origin and what they communicate is believed to add to our wisdom, and help us act more effectively in our universe.

Igbo Voices; hidden wisdom from the ancient language.

Introduction

The Igbo people are one of the most prominent ethnic groups in Africa
with a primary homeland in the South Eastern area of Nigeria.
The Igbos also live in surrounding countries most notably Cameroun,
Gabon and Equatorial Guinea.
They constitute significant numbers in many countries around the world
especially the United States, the United Kingdom and other major
economic hubs of the world.
Igbo(the language) is tonal and verb based.
In other words, Igbo is an action based language.
Each word is intended to convey a certain action or motion.
But because a thought or spirit always precedes any given action, Igbo
can be considered a spiritual language.

In this work we are performing etymological analysis of Igbo words.
By looking at the components or roots of each word; we are
looking at the action or motion a word conveys. We are also looking
at the spirit(or thought)before each word.
The Igbo language was designed to create a system of communication that
enables individuals participate and gain competence in their environment by
matching words with certain actions. This creates a system of communication
that allows individuals to express themselves without the use of force.

The words are arranged like a tree. Verbs are used to create word branches
carrying closely related words.
For example, the verb 'wu' carries such words such as iwu (law),
Owu (agony), and nwute (prolonged agony).

This work is intended to provide you with the skeleton of the system.

The word Igbo is derived from "I"(a prefix used as a verb/noun intensifier)
and "gbo"(prevent, guard). The verb or action word here is to guard.
Originally the Igbo's were intended to be guards.

At the time of writing, it is not clear to most people what the Igbo
were guarding, or if they lost something they were supposed to
protect.

Through this work I will endeavor to provide you with a glimpse.

Igbo Voices; hidden wisdom from the ancient language.

In this work, the Onitsha dialect is used. The author is only fluent in
the Onitsha dialect. Onitsha is an important trading post and was
once the largest single market in West Africa.

Igbo Voices; hidden wisdom from the ancient language.

Etymology of Igbo words

You will notice that many of these words are derivatives and fusion of other verbs or words. These words were engineered to resonate with each other, resonate with words for verbs and nouns in the physical and spiritual plane to the extent that the power of the individual words are amplified. We can describe this phenomenon as synergism.

The intention is to create a community were harmony is achieved not by whips, police or prisons, but by the power of the spoken word.

e, o, I, u , n, ọ,ụ, are prefixes used to propel/amplify/intensify a root

verb or a noun to varying degrees of intensity.

They are commonly placed before a noun/verb, but can also be placed after, as suffixes, as in di or du.

'a' is used to create the negative of the verb or noun. It is similar to the alpha derivative of ancient Greek. E.g. geometry and a-geometry (without geometry). Negative 'a' can be written as 'à'.
 It can also be used in a neutral manner in front of a verb or noun.

'e' is used to muffle the power of a verb or noun or create a partial negative.

'I' is a verb/noun intensifier.

'U' is a verb/noun intensifier often when referring to a group of people(community).

'N' is a verb/noun intensifier

'O' is used personally as an intensifier.

In some cases, there are slight phonological differences between nouns and verbs. The principle of approximation is used in these cases, e.g. the earth is not a true sphere but acts like one. So when NASA scientists make calculations regarding the earth they use sphere equations. And it checks out right. This is how approximation works.

So let's begin!

Igbo Voices; hidden wisdom from the ancient language.

The Words

"A" words: In these group of words "a" creates the negative.

'a' can also function in a neutral manner in a few words.

English:	Night
Igbo:	Abani
Breakdown:	"a" "ba"(enter) "ani"(land) "a" is a negative prefix.
Comments:	Night as a time not to venture into the farm, land or town. Be watchful of dangerous people and animals.

English:	Ada(name)
Igbo:	Ada
Breakdown:	"a" "da"(fall) "a" creates the negative
Comments:	Name given to first daughter. Prevents the fall of the family. Prevents the fall of the Obi (house) as in Adaobi. The action of the first daughter is to prevent the fall of her fathers and husbands household.

English:	Belly
Igbo:	Afọ
Breakdown:	"a" & "fọ" (remain) "a" creates the negative
Comments:	Big belly as that which causes early death or that which prevents you from remaining standing. This word is warning us of the dangers of a poor diet and that the development of a pot belly can lead to a number of medical conditions. Abdominal obesity is associated with hypertension/diabetes/obesity/Syndrome X/cancer and other medical conditions that may cause early mortality. See also ọffọr (ọfọ).

Igbo Voices; hidden wisdom from the ancient language.

English:	Suffering
Igbo:	Afụfụ
Breakdown:	"a" negative prefix and "fụ"(painful) and "fụ" (painful)
Comments:	Suffering as a state characterized as painless painfulness. Suffering is all in the mind. Suffering will yield joy, happiness and painlessness later!

English:	Afulenu(name)
Igbo:	Afuluenu
Breakdown:	afulu(seen) enu(sky)
Comments:	When a beautiful child comes into the family you might consider this name. 'we have seen the sky' is a way to acknowledge that God has given us part of his majesty and glamor.

English:	Hunger
Igbo:	Agụlụ
Breakdown:	"a"(negative prefix) "gụlụ"(to count)
Comments:	Living in a context of lack (spiritual and physical). A person who is hungry has nothing to count. No food stock or livestock or money to count. This individual has nothing to count on. One way of preventing hunger or scarcity is to keep an accurate count of your possessions. This is a way to master your possessions so you can cause them to increase.

English:	Pagan prosperity deity
Igbo:	Agwụ
Breakdown:	"a"("gwụ"-finish)
Comments:	That which cannot finish-a source of abundance.

Igbo Voices; hidden wisdom from the ancient language.

English:	Questioning
Igbo:	Ajụjụ
Breakdown:	a(neutral prefix) jụ(no) ju(no)
Comments:	Questioning is a way of repeatedly saying 'no' to whatever an individual is communicating. This could be due to omissions or commissions in the communication of the person being questioned. For example, a police man who is playing soccer, in uniform, could be questioned by a civilian if he was a policeman. This is a way of saying 'no' to what the irresponsible policeman is communicating.

English:	Bag
Igbo:	Akpa
Breakdown:	"a"&" kpa"(burden, bother)
Comments:	"a" creates the negative-that which prevents something or items from being burdensome. A bag is a way to put things together so they are not bothersome or difficult to carry.

English:	Kidney
Igbo:	Akụ
Breakdown:	"a"(negative prefix) "kụ"(to knock or break down)
Comments:	That which prevents the body from breaking down. The kidney plays critical metabolic and hormonal roles that prevents the body from breaking down.

Igbo Voices; hidden wisdom from the ancient language.

English:	Breast
Igbo:	Ala
Breakdown:	"A"(negative prefix) and "la"(to lick)
Comments:	Ala (breast) is derived from the verb la (to lick). Basically, the breast is 'commanding' to be licked by a baby or a lover. Breast feeding helps prevent numerous illnesses, and has numerous advantages. It is the best food for a newborn and promotes maternal bonding.

English:	Abomination
Igbo:	Alụ
Breakdown:	a "lụ"(to make, to work or create)
Comments:	To undo or destroy something made. "a" creates the negative. Society is like a machine with many gears working towards a common goal. To commit an abomination is to destroy this machinery. Fortunately, an abomination can be repaired through God's grace.

English:	Prophesy
Igbo:	Amụma
Breakdown:	"a" & "ma"(to know) ụma(to know)--here "a" also creates the negative. U is an amplifier/intensifier.
Comments:	To know the future without current knowledge. This word suggests that all a prophet does is to create a future situation by word of mouth. This is commonly an individual, with an exceptional knowledge of God and society that can capture a future condition in 'words'.

Igbo Voices; hidden wisdom from the ancient language.

English:	Earth
Igbo:	Ana
Breakdown:	a "na"(to go)
Comments:	"a" creates the negative; that which does not go away. The earth or land as something permanent. Our earth is permanent.

English:	Animal(Wild animal)
Igbo:	Anụ
Breakdown:	"a" & "nụ"(listen)
Comments:	That which does not listen. Here "a" also creates the negative. A wild animal cannot listen or obey your command. Distinguish this from domesticated animals not used for food.

English:	Happiness
Igbo:	Añuli
Breakdown:	Añu(honey) li(eat)
Comments:	Eating honey brings us to an emotional state that approximates happiness. We know that when we feel emotionally low, we tend to uplift ourselves with sugar rich foods such as chocolate. Unfortunately, this type of 'happiness' is temporary and may expose us to addiction to these sugar rich foods. Fortunately, there are natural things we can do to raise our emotional state such as engaging in a sporting activity. When we are truly happy, we feel like we have 'eaten honey', even though we haven't.

English:	Animal
Igbo:	Anụmana
Breakdown:	"anụ"(meat,flesh/animal), "ma"(to know) "ana"(land)
Comments:	A lower being that knows only the way of the earth or land. not in tune with God or the heavens.

Igbo Voices; hidden wisdom from the ancient language.

English:	Sun
Igbo:	Anwụ
Break down:	"a"("nwụ"-to die)
Comments:	"a" creates the negative-that which does not die. The sun does not die, slumber or sleeps. The sun is not like humans whose physical bodies' lives and subsequently dies. The Igbo know the earth turns around itself and the sun, hence the statement; ụwa na eme ntụ hari.

English:	Eye
Igbo:	Anya
Breakdown:	a(negative) "nya"(it, as is). Anya is 'not it' or 'not as is'
Comments:	This is a powerful one. This word is illustrating that the eye only creates mental image pictures. It is not the real thing or the complete 'picture'. We should experience what we see with our other senses. Do not judge a book by its cover. Also do not be carried away or be unduly influenced by what the eye sees.

English:	Night
Igbo:	Anyasi
Breakdown:	"anya"(eye) "si"(stop
Comments:	Time to close the eyes. Night as time to rest the eyes. This allows the brain to adjust from the entire stimulus it receives while the eyes are open.

English:	my body
Igbo:	arụ mụ
Breakdown:	arụ (body) mụ (my soul)
Comments:	I am not my body. It is just the covering of my soul. See also onwe mu(owner of my soul-my spirit).

Igbo Voices; hidden wisdom from the ancient language.

English:	Spit
Igbo:	Asọ
Breakdown:	a "sọ"(to respect) a creates the negative.
Comments:	To disrespect, to deconsecrate. See also nsọ- reverence.

D words.

English:	Forgive, forgiveness
Igbo:	"Di", "die", "Idi"
Breakdown:	d(to be, state of existing whole and complete)i(is an intensifier)
Comments:	To forgive is to be the person you were pre-mental injury or emotional assault. To forgive is to recover emotionally and psychological to the point that you are who you were before the challenge.
	This also means that you recover completely to your original state so that a repeat of the challenge is not possible.

Igbo Voices; hidden wisdom from the ancient language.

E words

English:	Dance, Game(play)
Igbo:	Egwu
Breakdown:	e(prefix used as a partial negative gwu (to protect). See ugwu (hill)
Comments:	Dance is basically a game. The purpose of a game is to protect our spirit so we can play more games. Igbo understands that life is like a game with goals and barriers. Although we may experience major painful events like the death of a loved one, but life remains basically like a game. Sometimes we get disillusioned and give up our dreams and goals, because we have judged the barriers insurmountable. We may feel like we are playing against a major football athlete. Dance (egwu) is a game (egwu) that can rehabilitate and protect our spirit so we can get back into the game of life. We naturally tend to break into a dance when we score a goal in a sport (notice the hard work required to score a goal), because dance is naturally linked to achieving goals. When we dance frequently, we would probably score more goals, in sports and in general life.

English:	Pumpkin soup
Igbo:	Egwusi
Breakdown:	"Egwu"(play) "si"(stop)
Comments:	When this soup is ready, it's time for the game (of life) to stop so we can feed. Egwusi soup is communicating 'timeout'. But after this meal, the game continues.

English:	Prayer
Igbo:	Ekpele
Breakdown:	"e" " kpe"(report) "le"(happen, actualize, manifest)
Comments:	Prayer as a habit of partial 'reporting' of issues to God but rather a focus on actualization of the request. 'E' creates a partial negative (muffling). Prayer in Igbo is in agreement with the Nike ad "Just do it". In Igbo; you kneel and meditate. Do not whine to God like a little kid. Go out there and "just do it!!" See also knee (Ikpele).

Igbo Voices; hidden wisdom from the ancient language.

English:	Sky, heavens.
Igbo:	Enu
Breakdown:	"e"& "nu"(nudge, push)
Comments:	That which nudges or motivates. A gentle push. 'E' is a muffler (partial positive) in this case. Want to get motivated; always look up.

English:	Eri(name of Igbo Spiritual Leader)
Igbo:	Eri
Breakdown:	"e" "ri"(leak, flow or reach out)
Comments:	"e"-creates a partial negative- This is a spiritual leader who causes the gentle flow of love and other spiritually related materials. See also Nri (town and civilization headquarters)

I words

English:	Love
Igbo:	Ifunanya.
Breakdown:	I fu(to see) na(in) anya(eye)
Comments:	Love is a very interesting topic. In Igbo love is very simple. People in love see things, basically, in the same way. So if they see a painting, they tend to agree as to whether that painting is good or bad. They see things as if they 'borrowed' each other's eyes. They are often in agreement in what they see or perceive. The stronger the agreement, the stronger the love. People in love like to talk about their perceptions and experiences. Because they have a high level of agreement, they validate each other's perceptions and experiences. This validation increases the love.

Igbo Voices; hidden wisdom from the ancient language.

English:	Igbo(people)
Igbo:	Igbo
Breakdown:	I gbo(prevent, protect, guard,)
Comments:	I is an intensifier. An Igbo is a Guard. What are they guarding? See also Ugbo To be Igbo is to live a protected life. Protected by God, and a witness to God's protection.

English:	Power
Igbo:	Ike
Breakdown:	I(positive prefix) ke(create)
Comments:	Power is creation. Power is the ability to create. An individual with power is able to change the physical universe into a desired structure such as buildings. They can create jobs. They have wide powers to create. Sometimes individuals in power can create war that leads to suffering and destruction. Unfortunately, that ugly situation is still a creation.

English:	Knee
Igbo:	Ikpele
Breakdown:	I kpe(report, confess, reveal) le(manifest, actualize)
Comments:	The knee appears to be an important spiritual tool for prayer (ekpele). They are most probably derived from the same words and the two should go hand in hand. "I" is an intensifier, it appears that when one performs a prayer with the knees to the ground the power of the prayer is intensified. Basically, after prayer, the knee is what is used to carry the body to a location where the prayer is actualized. The knee is a major weight bearing joint in the body, and free movement is not possible without a healthy knee.

Igbo Voices; hidden wisdom from the ancient language.

English:	Tongue
Igbo:	Ile
Breakdown:	I (positive prefix) and le (manifest)
Comments:	We all know there is power in the spoken word, and we are All familiar with the phrase "watch your tongue". What we say plays a strong role in creating our universe.

J words

English:	Yam
Igbo:	Ji
Breakdown:	Ji (hold, holder)
Comments:	Yam is a specialist in converting and storing the energy of the Sun in the form of complex carbohydrates in its tuber. Yam accomplishes this, in a relatively short period, by utilizing a comparatively thin stem and branches. The carbohydrates in yam are digested slowly by the human body such that the glucose yielded is released gradually into the blood stream over a prolonged period compared to potatoes, rice or other common staples. This is a favorable glycemic index. When an individual eats yam the energy is prolonged and sustained. Yam is very good for physical and demanding jobs and ill patients.

English:	Question
Igbo:	Jụ
Breakdown:	jụ (no)
Comments:	when you question someone you are basically saying 'no' to whatever they are communicating. Either because there are omissions in their communication or the subject was not properly communicated. An individual questioning you is basically saying no to what you are communicating. jụ is also the word for cold. Being cold to someone is a way of saying 'no' to them. An object that is cold is also saying 'no'. See also questioning-ajụjụ

Igbo Voices; hidden wisdom from the ancient language.

K words.

English:	Star
Igbo:	kpakpando
Breakdown:	kpa kpa(ruffle, scatter, border, burden), ndo(shade, shield, canopy, roof)
Comments:	That which scatters the shield or shade. It is believed that the sky and the clouds are a shield or shade that protects the earth from the powerful rays of the sun and stars(see also ozone layer) The light of the stars are powerful enough to scatter that shield and hence their light reaches us (kpakpando). Without the shield, there will be no night as the light from billions of stars will illuminate the earth at night. The sun is powerful enough to penetrate the shield completely and produce daylight. Sunset provides a powerful illustration of the power of the ndo (the sky and the clouds). Notice that the sky and clouds are able to shield us from the power of the sun at sunset to the point that you can gaze at the sun. This is impossible at mid-day. For a while after sunset, the sky illuminates from the energy it trapped from the sun (in much the same way as the leaves of a tree trap light). The energy is released as light and the beautiful coloring is a function of the gases illuminated. When much of the light energy is dispensed, the light of the stars become powerful enough to 'ruffle', break through the sky and clouds and reach us as kpakpando.

M words.

Mbọ -revenge

Mbọlu-making revenge.

Revenge is a very important subject in every culture and spirituality. If we look at revenge in Christianity we note that a certain action is prescribed. Moses had recommended an eye for an eye (tit for tat). This action must have been examined and upheld by many prophets that followed Moses

Igbo Voices; hidden wisdom from the ancient language.
like Jeremiah, Nehemiah, Elijah, and even John the Baptist. To the dismay of his fellow Hebrews, Jesus overturned the law and recommended 'turn the other cheek'. The action Jesus had recommended for revenge was the very opposite of 'tit for tat'. Jesus wanted us to show love to our enemies.

But how did the ancient Igbo's consider revenge? What action did they prescribe as revenge? How should we revenge? The answer to that question lies in the Igbo word for revenge 'mbọ'. Igbo as we know, is a verb based language. The word mbọ contains a verb or action word that denotes revenge.

Before we go into that verb or action word, I would like us to consider two closely related words. These words are closely related morphologically, semantically, and phonetically but are words for different subjects.

The first is 'mbọ'; which is the word for nail(s).

The second is 'mbọ' which is the word for hard or effective work.

So what do nails, effective work and revenge have in common?

How could these three entirely different subjects share a common motion or action?

To understand ancient Igbo; I would like to tell you a short story. You can call it a parable if you choose.

"In ancient times the Igbo were primarily an agricultural society; most people were farmers.

On one cool but sunny day, a prominent spiritual man was recalled to his house due to an emergency. As he approached his house, he noticed a small silent crowd. He was beckoned towards his house. As he entered he heard moans and groans emanating from his bedroom. He walked closer and as he opened the door he noticed a trusted friend on top of his wife.

Igbo Voices; hidden wisdom from the ancient language.
Being spiritual and strong he had a larger than normal hoe which he brought with him from the farm.

His grip hardened as rage diverted blood away from the centers of the brain that governed reasoning.

But from his spirit he heard the Igbo word for revenge; mbọ, mbọ, mbọ.

So he stepped back, turned around, and walked increasingly faster out of the house and towards the farm, then he broke into a sprint. When he got into the farm, he dug, dug, dug. He enriched mounds, made new ones, and removed weeds. When he finished, the Sun was setting and when he looked at his farm it was very beautiful. It was as if he had made a new hair style on mother earth, and mother earth was smiling.

When he got back home, his house was empty. He was soon joined by a young lady who was very impressed by his action and asked him why he did not kill the man adding that 'everyone would understand'. The Nze (a spiritual leader meaning to shield) replied, 'there is nothing to be impressed about'. What I have done has been repeatedly performed by men before me. He brought some palm wine out, and served the lady. 'Chinyere (her name)" he said; 'notice that I am not cleaning up blood, and I would not be facing the elders to determine if my actions are justified or not". "you see our word for revenge mbọ is derived from bọ which is the verb to dig". "We revenge by going back to work to dig, and dig deeper. "That is the ultimate revenge", he said.

The verb bọ is used in the word for nail (mbọ) because the nail is used for digging (animals) or women use it to dig into the skin of their lovers. 'Bọ' is also the action word for hard work (mbo) because in an agricultural society the only way to work hard and effective is dig, dig, dig (deeper). Dig out the weeds that compete with your crops for nutrients. Weeds are barriers to success.

Igbo Voices; hidden wisdom from the ancient language.

In Igbo, the prescribed action for revenge (mbọ) is to dig deeper into your work, digging out the barriers (weeds) to success; whether you are a farmer, doctor, lawyer, nurse or a shoe maker.

The goals of a human being in a good mental condition should not include revenge against any group or person.

English:	Stone, especially heavy stone.
Igbo:	Mkpume
Breakdown:	mkpu (to mold) and ume (strength or breath)
Comments:	Heavy stone for weight training. It can mold your strength. Lie on a flat piece of rock and note how it molds your strength.

English:	Beauty, good.
Igbo:	Mma
Breakdown:	mma is to know.
Comments:	Beauty is a statement of good knowledge. A beautiful car is a statement of good knowledge of cars. A beautiful woman is an expression of good knowledge of femininity. Knowledge is good or beautiful.

English:	Human Being, Important human being.
Igbo:	Mmadụ
Breakdown:	mma + "n"dụ. To know life.
Comments:	mma (to know) " n"dụ is, exists, lives, alive). In Igbo land, an mmadụ (human being, important human being) is a person 'who knows how life is'. This person knows how life works and is a very good resource when a solution is sought. See also beauty (mma).

Igbo Voices; hidden wisdom from the ancient language.

English:	Palm Oil, oil.
Igbo:	mmanụ.
Breakdown:	mma (beautiful, knowledge) +nụ (is)
Comments:	Knowledge about oil is very important in creating a beautiful life. Oils are not just important as creams to oil our skins; they are also important food items. The palm oil is so priced that even the Pharaohs were buried with a portion for use in the afterlife. Today, evidence is pouring out regarding the benefits of oils(including fish oil) in a wide range of medical conditions. Palm oil is very beautiful oil.

English:	Alcohol
Igbo:	mmanya.
Breakdown:	mma (beauty) + nya (it)
Comments:	That which is the beauty of it. The beauty of the palm tree is that it can make palm wine (alcohol). The beauty of barley is that we can turn it into beer (alcohol). Alcohol played a key role in the earliest human civilizations. Be careful when you drink alcohol because it distorts realty and make things more beautiful than they seem.

English:	Water
Igbo:	mmiri
Breakdown:	mmi(deep) + ri(leak, reach out, flow).
Comments:	Water as deep flowing. Water is indispensable for survival and is truly deep flowing. When we drink water it is quickly absorbed and distributed around the body. The same is true for water as rain, river, sea or ocean. It is deep flowing.

Igbo Voices; hidden wisdom from the ancient language.

English:	Masquerade
Igbo:	mmọnwụ
Breakdown:	mma + onwụ
Comments:	mma (good, beautiful), onwụ (death)- that which beautifies death. Masquerades are often called to perform during burial ceremonies. They are supposedly the spirit of a departed ancestor. Their agility, dance, and movements suggest that though one is dead physically, they are very much alive and active in the spiritual plane.

English:	My soul or mind
Igbo:	Mụ
Breakdown:	Mụ
Comments:	The soul is what we use to compute everyday problems. onwe mụ (owner of my soul) is the spirit. See also my body(arụ mụ).

N words.

English:	Patience
Igbo:	Ndidi
Breakdown:	N di (to be) di (to be)
Comments:	Patience as a state of being your true self and remaining your true self despite unfavorable environmental challenges. The person who is patient does not respond negatively to unfavorable personal circumstances. Stand your ground and be strong like a tree. Do not whine. Be resistant to wire-brushing. Be of service, and whether the storm.

Igbo Voices; hidden wisdom from the ancient language.

English:	Sorry
Igbo:	Ndo
Breakdown:	N (verb intensifier) and udo (peace)
Comments:	To pacify; this word is the application of peace to someone. This word is also related to ndo (shelter). To say sorry (ndo) is to bring peace into the consciousness of the offended.

English:	Lungs
Igbo:	Ngụgụ
Breakdown:	n (positive prefix) and gụgụ (heal or console)
Comments:	We can use our lungs to console or heal ourselves. There is scientific evidence that when we slow our breath to about 3-6 cycles per minute, after 10 minutes, we begin to feel a sense of well being. This is useful for stress, anxiety, depression, worry, post-traumatic stress disorder, phobias, pain, and respiratory problems.

English:	Wing(of birds)
Igbo:	Nkuku
Breakdown:	n(positive prefix) ku(air movement) and ku (air movement)
Comments:	The wings of a bird are used to create repeated air movements that cause flight.

English:	Tools
Igbo:	Ngwọlụ
Breakdown:	ngwọ (healing, making good) and olụ (work)
Comments:	Tools are what we use to do a good job. Or we use tools for 'making good' a work assignment. So it is important that we select the tools that we need to do a good job timely.

Igbo Voices; hidden wisdom from the ancient language.

English:	Father
Igbo:	Nna
Breakdown:	n(privative)na(a variant of supervision)
Comments:	'na' is related to 'ne' which refers to see or oversee. A father is an overseer but it appears that this job function is made possible by the presence or activity of a mother(nne).

English:	Mother
Igbo:	Nne
Breakdown:	n(prefix)ne(see or oversee)
Comments:	The mother is a general overseer of the house. Oversees the children and the father as well. The father and mother are co-overseers.

English:	slow, slowly
Igbo:	nwayo
Breakdown:	nwa(child) yọ(shake)
Comments:	This word captures the gentle motion that is used to soothe a child. When one does something slowly, one is approximating this gentle motion.

English:	Nri (Igbo Kingdom)
Igbo:	Nri
Breakdown:	N(ri)- to reach out, leak out or flow.
Comments:	Living in a context of the need for spiritual food. Nri was created to lighten the burden of mankind through spiritual techniques in much the same way as Christianity. Nri was also advanced in farming techniques and in ancient times was an agricultural research and development site. Nri developed and delivered spiritual techniques that flowed around Igbo land and neighboring states.

English:	Poison
Igbo:	Nsi
Breakdown:	N si (stop) N is an intensifier
Comments:	Poison as something that can stop a human, animal or other living things.

English:	Trouble
Igbo:	nsogbu
Breakdown:	nso(following) gbu(pain)
Comments:	Trouble seems to arise when we consciously or sub-consciously follow pain. It is possible that a previously emotionally painful incident is misdirecting us towards 'trouble' without our knowledge.

English:	Reverence
Igbo:	nsọ
Breakdown:	n (prefix) sọ (respect or reverence.)
Comments:	see asọ (spit)

English:	Stupidity, moronic behavior
Igbo:	nsọkwu
Breakdown:	nsọ(respect, reverence) kwu(speech)
Comments:	Stupid people have a reverence for words. They are at the command of other peoples words. If you tell them to 'come over here'. They sheepishly come. If you tell them, 'they are stupid'; they act stupid. These people can easily be manipulated with words. A word like the 'n' word can drive them into uncontrollable rage. Fortunately, the Igbo have the technology to deactivate the words.

Igbo Voices; hidden wisdom from the ancient language.

English:	Nwosu(name)
Igbo:	Nwosu
Breakdown:	nwa (son) and osu (an ancient deity that can invoke the ancestors)
Comments;	This is the child of a deity that can invoke the ancestors.

English:	Shepherd Priest.
Igbo:	Nze
Breakdown:	N ze (to protect)
Comments:	Lower level priest serves as a protector, guardian or shepherd of the masses. They are trained by ọzọ priests.

English:	Salvation
Igbo:	Nzọpụta
Breakdown:	nzọ (to save) pụta (outing)
Comments:	Salvation is saving out an individual from death or destruction.

English:	Stepping out
Igbo:	Nzọpụta
Breakdown:	Nzọ (stepping) pụta (out)
Comments:	This may be related to salvation because personal action is required in salvation. The first action is stepping out of one's comfort zone in a Church or religious venue to receive salvation.

Igbo Voices; hidden wisdom from the ancient language.

O words.

English:	Barn
Igbo:	ọba (as in ọba ji-barn for yams)
Breakdown:	ọ (privative) ba (from banye (enter)
Comments:	That which is a space for something. Space or reservoir

English:	Heart
Igbo:	Obi
Breakdown:	O bi (to live, to be alive) O is an intensifier used in personal terms.
Comments:	That which makes you live. One dies when the heart stops. This demonstrates a practical Igbo understanding of anatomy and physiology.

English:	Chair
Igbo:	Oche
Breakdown:	O che (guard, wait)
Comments:	A chair is used to wait, and guards a person from falling to the ground.

English:	Igbo staff of Authority.
Igbo:	ọffọr (ọfọ)
Break down:	ọ (privative) fọ (to remain)
Comments:	The ọffọr is the Igbo staff of authority. It is derived from a branch of a special tree. The holder of an ọfọ is expected to speak the truth at all times. The truth is what sets us free. It is symbolic, and derived from the fact that the branches of a tree cause it to remain standing. The person who speaks the truth will remain standing. Be like a tree; branch out or diversify. Do not depend on one primary branch for survival. When you are diversified you will not be afraid to speak the truth for fear of losing a job or a relationship.

Igbo Voices; hidden wisdom from the ancient language.

English:	Gong
Igbo:	Ogene
Breakdown:	O ge(time) and ene(watch)
Comments:	The gong is used to draw the community to listen and watch on different occasions. Ogene is time to listen and watch.

English:	Black(person or object)
Igbo:	Oji
Breakdown:	O(personal intensifier) and ji(holder, reservoir, absorber)
Comments:	A black object or person absorbs light and is therefore a holder or absorber of light/energy. A black person as a holder of something. A black person always retains something.

English:	Ojukwu (name).
Igbo:	Ojukwu
Breakdown:	Oju (filled up) ukwu (a lot, plenty)
Comments:	The bearer of this name is a stand for abundance. He is a means for abundance in his community.

English:	Fire
Igbo:	ọkụ
Breakdown:	"ọ " Community privative and "kụ"-breakdown
Comments:	Fire as that which breaks down! Be it food item or a house, etc.

English:	Foot
Igbo:	ọkpa
Breakdown:	ọkpa (to scatter, shuffle)—see stars (kpakpando)
Comments:	Used for animals-that which is used to shuffle the earth.

Igbo Voices; hidden wisdom from the ancient language.

English:	Cap, Hat
Igbo:	Okpu
Breakdown:	O (prefix) kpu (to cover)
Comments:	cap or hat is a covering. The purpose of a hat is to cover the hair/head. It is a sign of humility and submission to God.

English:	Bone
Igbo:	ọkpụkpụ
Breakdown:	ọ(prefix) kpụ (mold), kpụ (mold)
Comments:	Bone as the mold in which the body is molded from.

English:	Temple(Church)
Igbo:	Okwu
Breakdown:	O kwu (speak)
Comments:	Temple as a place where the Supreme being speaks or where men (or woman) speak about the Supreme being.

English:	Faith
Igbo:	Okwukwe
Breakdown:	okwu (word), kwe (agree)
Comments:	To have faith is to agree with the word of God. Agree with God's word and it will be well with you. In all religions, we notice that God has kind words for us. He has plans for us even when we remain sinners. All we have to do is to agree with his word to have a good life.

Igbo Voices; hidden wisdom from the ancient language.

English:	Stone
Igbo:	Okwute
Breakdown:	Okwu (to speak) and te (long)
Comments:	A stone as an instrument you can use in making a statement over a prolonged period of time. When you build on stone, it offers you an opportunity to make a statement over countless generations. You can also carve in messages into the stone for posterity. Just like the ancient Egyptians did.

English:	Behavior
Igbo:	Omume
Breakdown:	o mu (me) me(maker, doer)
Comments:	Behavior; I am the doer/maker. Each individual should take responsibility for their behavior as an individual's behavior is a personal creation. We have to ensure that our behavior is consistent with the life we are trying to create.

English:	Jewelry
Igbo:	ọna
Breakdown:	ọna (to go)
Comments:	Jewelry is temporary it comes and goes. See ana (land, earth)

English:	Mouth
Igbo:	ọnụ
Breakdown:	ọ (prefix) nụ (listen)
Comments:	That which creates that which you listen to. The mouth is also a listening tool. Sound actually reaches the inner ears through the teeth and jaw bones. Technology to listen to sound through the mouth has recently been developed to treat patients with conductive hearing loss. It is placed on the upper palate.The verb nụ is also used to describe the act or ceremony in which a man marries a woman. Marriage is a listening or communication contract between two parties. When the communication is good, there is more love.

Igbo Voices; hidden wisdom from the ancient language.

English:	Voice
Igbo:	Onu
Breakdown:	O nu (push)
Comments:	Voice of a people creates language or words that can push issues that are a concern for that group. See also enu (sky)

English:	Neck
Igbo:	Onu
Breakdown:	O nu (push) also voice
Comments:	The voice box in the neck is a very important structure. Without it we cannot adequately communicate and we will have a hard time pushing matters of importance.

English:	My spirit
Igbo:	onwe mụ
Breakdown:	onwe (owner) mụ (my soul)
Comments:	The spirit is the owner of my soul or my mind. I am not my body. I am not my soul. I am my spirit. My spirit uses my soul and body to do the tasks it chooses.

English:	Trap
Igbo:	ọnya.
Breakdown:	ọ (prefix) nya (to carry or drive)
Comments:	a trap can seize an animal for you to carry away later.

Igbo Voices; hidden wisdom from the ancient language.

English:	Person
Igbo:	Onye
Breakdown:	O (prefix) nye (giver)
Comments:	O is used personally as an intensifier. A person is a giver. People should live in the context that they are givers. Everything alive is providing a service to someone or something else. E.g. a tree provides a service by making a fruit for a monkey, and the monkey disperses the seed of the fruit on behalf of the tree. Every individual should be providing some service or good.

English:	Moon
Igbo:	ọnwa
Breakdown:	ọ(prefix) nwa(child)
Comments:	The moon as a child of the earth. The moon is a breakaway piece of the earth. The moon is also like a child. It starts small as the new moon, and then grows to its full size, before fading. This transient and mobile nature of the moon gives us a perspective when we deal with our children. We have to understand that our relationship with our children is like the earth and the moon. We can influence our children but they have a degree of autonomy.

English:	One, 1
Igbo:	Otu
Breakdown:	O(prefix) tu(oneness or togetherness)
Comments:	The number one represents wholeness or togetherness.

Igbo Voices; hidden wisdom from the ancient language.

English:	Group, peer group.
Igbo:	Otu
Breakdown:	O(prefix) tu(togetherness, oneness)
Comments:	A group is about creating togetherness or oneness. The purpose of a group is to act like one. This is a way to leverage power. If you are having trouble achieving a goal, try joining a group and leverage your power.

English:	Praise, praise worship
Igbo:	Otuto
Breakdown:	otu(group) to(praise)
Comments:	Praise is an oneness activity to recognize an individual or God. A church choir is basically 'group praise'.

English:	Vagina
Igbo:	ọtụ
Breakdown:	ọ (prefix) tụ (to charm, draw or magnetize) Here ọ is a prefix used for personal issues.
Comments:	The vagina is very charming and one can get magnetized. There are natural ways to increase the charm of the vagina. Shaving, trimming, or styling vaginal hair may be a good start.

English:	Cold
Igbo:	Oyi
Breakdown:	o (prefix) yi (wear)
Comments:	Cold makes us wear clothing (much). See also yi (wear) and note that to wear clothing is a way to 'look like' the clothing you are wearing.

Igbo Voices; hidden wisdom from the ancient language.

English:	Saviour Priest (Ozo)
Igbo:	ọzọ
Breakdown:	ọ(prefix) zọ (to save)
Comments:	High priest who saves.

English:	Corpse
Igbo:	Ozu
Breakdown:	O (verb intensifier used on personal issues), zu (completion, thief)
Comments:	When someone dies what remains is the corpse. The corpse represents a 'completion' of the cycle of life for the individual. The corpse is the 'thief' or 'retainer' of the spirit, which escapes when an individual dies. When an individual is alive, the body (the thief) prevents the true essence of the spirit from manifesting. Prayer and meditation are spiritual tools used to tame the body so the true essence of the spirit is brought to light in one's life time, as much as possible.

S words.

English:	Crouch
Igbo:	Sekpuluana
Breakdown:	se (draw) kpulu (cover) ana (earth)
Comments:	In everyday speech, we translate this word as kneeling but it is a different posture. This is the posture one assumes when an individual is trying to pray. In this position, after kneeling, the head is bowed to the same level as the ground or bed. It looks like the person is covering the earth, or is like a 'hat' over the earth. Note that Okpu (hat) is from kpu (cover).

Igbo Voices; hidden wisdom from the ancient language.

T words.

English:	Title
Igbo:	tu
Breakdown:	tu (oneness) see from the number one (otu)
Comments:	The purpose of a title is to create oneness between ourselves and the title. For example, an individual whose title is 'Lion' is trying to achieve oneness with a lion. The goal is to act like a lion.

U words.

English:	Wealth
Igbo:	ụba
Breakdown:	ụ (prefix) ba (to enter, space for something to enter)
Comments:	Wealth is to have increased capacity. See also Barn (Oba). To be wealth is to be a reservoir. Wealthy people often have the ability to reach out to many people. They are directly or indirectly associated with a large number of people. They make and/or receive a large number of phone calls. To be wealthy, is to have a large capacity.

English:	Brain
Igbo:	ụbụru
Breakdown:	ụ (prefix) bụrụ (being)
Comments:	The use of the 'ụ' prefix suggests the brain has a community orientation. The brain should be for community use. Our brain gives us our 'being'. Our 'being' determines what we are going to specialize in as a profession.

English:	Thought(good thought), wisdom
Igbo:	Uche
Breakdown:	u(prefix) che(wait or guard)
Comments:	Thought is actually meditation by waiting. To think is to wait.

Igbo Voices; hidden wisdom from the ancient language.

English:	Igbo apple
Igbo:	ụdala
Breakdown:	ụda(to fall) and la(lick)
Comments:	When this exotic fruit falls, it is time to pick it up and lick or suck its delicious innards.

English:	Vulture
Igbo:	Udene
Breakdown:	Ude(prowl-hunt), ene(watch)
Comments:	That which prowl-hunts and watches.

English:	Farm, farming
Igbo:	Ugbo
Breakdown:	U (prefix) gbo (prevent, guarding)
Comments:	U is an intensifier often used when the activity refers to more than one person (community activity). Farming as a preventive measure. Farm today and eat tomorrow.

English:	Debt
Igbo:	ụgwọ
Breakdown:	ụ (prefix) gwọ (to heal or make good)
Comments:	Debt is what we use to 'make good' or heal a lender. Do not lend someone unreliable money because it could cause you distress that can result to illness.

Igbo Voices; hidden wisdom from the ancient language.

English:	Hill
Igbo:	Ugwu
Breakdown:	U (community prefix) gwu (to build a protection)
Coments:	We use the verb 'gwu' to communicate the digging motion that creates a mound. The purpose of a mound is to protect a seed from the elements and from seed eaters such as birds. So we can translate the verb gwu as protection, making hill (ugwu) the creation of a protection. In early times, people often settled on hills because it provided protection against flood and fierce storms. A hill is also easier to defend compared to lower ground. Because the hill looks like a huge mound, it would appear it was created by a god or God. So the hill helped develop early beliefs in the existence of God. So you can understand why the Psalmist says, 'I look up unto the hills, from whence does my help come'. (Psalm 121).

English:	Church
Igbo:	ụka
Breakdown:	ụ (prefix) ka (to talk or communicate)
Comments:	Church (or house of worship) as a place of talk or communication. A church provides a venue where members can communicate to each other about what God is doing in their lives.

English:	Grasshopper
Igbo:	ụkpana
Breakdown:	"ụkpa"(scavenger) "ana"(land)
Comments:	Grasshopper as scavenger of the land.

English:	Leg
Igbo:	ụkwụ
Breakdown:	ụ (prefix) kwụ (stand)
Comments:	That which is used to remain standing.

Igbo Voices; hidden wisdom from the ancient language.

English:	Well (water well)
Igbo:	ụmi
Breakdown:	ụ (prefix used in community issues and "mi"(to suck, suction)
Comments:	A well functions like a straw. When we suck on a straw placed into a drink, we create an area of negative pressure in the throat that forces the water up. A well functions on the same principle. When you dig a narrow channel into the ground, you are creating an area of negative pressure that forces water up into the well. All you have to do is to dig close to the underground water table, and then leave the rest to the suction pressure. This word suggests that these ancient people knew basic engineering principles.

English:	Sleep
Igbo:	ụla
Breakdown:	U (prefix used in community or multi-person occasions to enhance the power of a verb/noun and "la" (to go)
Comments:	Sleep as a way of' going away' to rest the brain and body. We should ensure we are getting adequate sleep. It is a 'holiday' we get every day, we often take for granted.

English:	Strength
Igbo:	Ume
Breakdown:	"u"(prefix used in community settings) and "me"(to do, make)
Comments:	Strength is required to do stuff or make thing happen.

English:	Liver
Igbo:	Umeju
Breakdown:	ume (strength) and ju (full)
Comments:	Energy store house-biochemically the liver is an energy storehouse. This illustrates an Igbo understanding of the role of the liver in the body.

Igbo Voices; hidden wisdom from the ancient language.

English:	Children
Igbo:	ụmụ
Breakdown:	ụ (community prefix) mụ (my soul)
Comments:	Children as a way an individual extends his soul in the community. It is good to have children because they serve as our ambassadors.

English:	Banana
Igbo:	Unere.
Breakdown:	'unọ'(house) 'ere'(to leak)
Comments:	Banana leaves can be used to fix roof leaks.

English:	Home
Igbo:	ụnọ
Breakdown:	ụ (community prefix used to intensify the power of a verb/noun) and 'nọ'-to be near or together
Comments:	Home is where people can be near one another or come together. The action a house communicates is togetherness. A house brings people together as a family.

English:	Mat
Igbo:	Ute
Breakdown:	U(prefix used in multiperson or community to intensify a verb) te(long or prolong)
Comments:	Lie on a mat next to the earth and your life will be prolonged. When you lie on a mat next to the earth, the latter absorbs bad energy from your body. The word for "lie down" which is 'di nọ ana' in Igbo illustrates the point. 'Di nọ ana' actually is translated 'be with the earth' or 'be near the earth'. David also makes a similar point in Psalm 23 when he says; ".....he makes me lie down in green pastures, he restores my soul". When you lie on a mat next to the earth, the earth takes away your illnesses, gives you more strength and restores your strength.

Igbo Voices; hidden wisdom from the ancient language.

English:	Contribution
Igbo:	ụtụ
Breakdown:	ụtụ (to throw, charm or hook) see also vagina (ọtụ)
Comments:	Contribution is a process in which people are sold an inspiring activity in a manner that compels them to throw in their support in the form of money or similar items.

English:	Way
Igbo:	ụzọ
Breakdown:	"ụ" community Prefix and "zọ"; step. zọ is also 'save'. See nzoputa (salvation)
Comments:	A road (way) is a way to save lives, time, etc. ụzọ (early morning) is a way to save the day! One of the facts the Igbo is communicating is that each time we take a step we are actually creating roads. ụzọ = way=stepping. This is because our saved steps create roads. This is obvious when you see a path created on grass by steps.

Y words.

English:	Wear
Igbo:	Yi
Breakdown:	Yi (resemble)
Comments:	When we wear clothing we are actually trying to resemble (or look like) the clothing we are wearing. Clothing is an opportunity for us to send messages to the outside world about any theme we would like to communicate.

Igbo Voices; hidden wisdom from the ancient language.

Conclusion

Igbo words are practical and are designed to help an individual gain competence in their universe. I hope you found this work useful. The writer does not believe this is the final or complete guide to the understanding of Igbo words. The writer hopes this will stimulate interest in the Igbo language. It is believed that understanding these words would help individuals gain and apply more wisdom.

I recommend that you read the book several times so you can draw your own conclusions. Many of the words convey very complex information that was deliberately shortened to make the book readable by a wide audience.

Hopefully, this book helped shift your understanding of the universe a little bit.

Igbo Voices; hidden wisdom from the ancient language.

The End

Igbo voices will return!

Igbo Voices; hidden wisdom from the ancient language.

Bibliography

1. Chikodi Anunobi. Nri Warriors of Peace. Zenith Press; 1 edition (February 28, 2006)
2. Chinua Achebe. Things Fall Apart. Anchor Books -- Doubleday, NYC (January 1, 1994)
3. Richard P. Brown M.D. and Patricia L. Gerbarg. The Healing Power of the breath. 2012 Shambhala publications.
4. Christopher Ejizu. Ofo; Igbo ritual and symbol. Fourth Dimension Publishing Co. (March 11, 2002)
5. Botha, R. and C. Knight (eds) 2009. *The Cradle of Language.* Oxford: Oxford University Press

Igbo Voices; hidden wisdom from the ancient language.

Index and Notes

Igbo Voices; hidden wisdom from the ancient language.

Igbo Voices; hidden wisdom from the ancient language.

Igbo Voices; hidden wisdom from the ancient language.

Igbo Voices; hidden wisdom from the ancient language.

Igbo Voices; hidden wisdom from the ancient language.

Igbo Voices; hidden wisdom from the ancient language.

Igbo Voices; hidden wisdom from the ancient language.